DINOSAURS!

SPINOSAURUS
AND OTHER DINOSAURS AND REPTILES FROM
THE UPPER CRETACEOUS

by
David West

Gareth Stevens
Publishing

Please visit our website, www.garethstevens.com.
For a free color catalog of all our high-quality books,
call toll free 1-800-542-2595 or fax 1-877-542-2596.

Library of Congress Cataloging-in-Publication Data

West, David, 1956-
Spinosaurus and other dinosaurs and reptiles from the upper Cretaceous / David West.
p. cm. — (Dinosaurs!)
Includes index.
ISBN 978-1-4339-6721-4 (pbk.)
ISBN 978-1-4339-6722-1 (6-pack)
ISBN 978-1-4339-6719-1 (library binding)
1. Spinosaurus—Juvenile literature. 2. Dinosaurs—Juvenile literature. 3. Reptiles, Fossil—Juvenile literature. 4. Paleontology—Cretaceous—Juvenile literature. I. Title.
QE862.S3W4665 2012
567.9—dc23
2011037695

First Edition

Published in 2012 by
Gareth Stevens Publishing
111 East 14th Street, Suite 349
New York, NY 10003

Copyright © 2012 David West Books

Designed by David West Books

Special thanks to Dr. Ron Blakey for the map on page 4

Printed in China

CPSIA compliance information: Batch #DW12GS: For further information contact Gareth Stevens, New York, New York at 1-800-542-2595.

Contents

Map labels: Western Interior Seaway · North America · LAURASIA · Asia · LARAMIDIA · APPALACHIA · Europe · Arabia · Southeast Asia · Central Atlantic Ocean · TETHYS SEA · Equator · South America · Africa · India · GONDWANA · Australia · Antarctica

This map shows what the world looked like around 90 million years ago.

The Upper Cretaceous Period

During the Upper Cretaceous, the climate was warmer than today, but it was gradually becoming cooler. As sea levels rose, the Western Interior Seaway divided North America into two parts, Appalachia and Laramidia. India continued to move northward as it separated from Madagascar. In the Southern Hemisphere, Australia and Antarctica remained connected as Africa and South America drifted apart.

*Dinosaurs lived throughout the Mesozoic Era, which is divided into three periods, shown here. It is sometimes called the Age of Reptiles. Dinosaurs first appeared in the Upper Triassic period and died out during a **mass extinction event** 65 million years ago.*

Giant **pterosaurs** and birds ruled the skies. Modern sharks appeared in the oceans.

LIFE DURING THE UPPER CRETACEOUS

This period saw many new types of dinosaurs appearing. The duckbills, **ankylosaurids**, and horned dinosaurs grew in numbers in North America and Asia. **Tyrannosaurids** were the major **predators** in North America. **Pachycephalosaurids** were also present in both North America and Asia, as were **dromaeosaurids**. **Therizinosaurids** were living only in Asia. Gondwana had very different dinosaurs, with most predators being **abelisaurids**. **Titanosaurids** were the dominant **herbivores** here. Birds, insects and plants became more common. **Mosasaurs** and **elasmosaurs** fed on the vast schools of fish. At the end of the Upper Cretaceous, 65% of all life—including all the dinosaurs— were wiped out in the Cretaceous-Tertiary extinction event.

227	200	180	159	144		98		65 *Millions of years ago (mya)*
Upper	*Lower*	*Middle*	*Upper*		*Lower*		*Upper*	
TRIASSIC		*JURASSIC*			*CRETACEOUS*			

Horseshoe Canyon

In a scene from Upper Cretaceous North America, a variety of dinosaurs gather near a river. **Fossil** evidence from the Horseshoe Canyon Formation shows a remarkable **diversity** of animals living in a cool, dry climate around 70 million years ago.

At the top of the food chain in this local **ecosystem** was the tyrannosaurid, *Albertosaurus*. It was a bipedal predator with tiny, two-fingered hands and a massive head with dozens of large, sharp teeth.

Albertosauruses (1) *chase a **juvenile** Pachyrhinosaurus, who runs for the safety of his herd (2). On the river edge,* Euoplocephaluses (3) *feed on succulent plants. A herd of* Edmontosauruses (4) *make their way to join* Saurolophuses (5) *feeding on river plants.*

Prey would have included any of the many plant eaters living at this time, including the duck-billed dinosaurs *Edmontosaurus* and *Saurolophus* as well as armored dinosaurs such as *Euoplocephalus* and *Edmontia*. Juveniles of the horned dinosaurs *Pachyrhinosaurus*, *Anchiceratops*, and *Arrhinoceratops* might also have been preyed upon.

Edmontosaurus grew up to 39 feet (11.9 m) long and weighed around 4.4 tons (4 metric tons).

Hell Creek

The Hell Creek Formation provides a glimpse of life during the Upper Cretaceous in North America. River deltas and swamplands on the edge of the Western Interior Seaway were home to some of the best-known dinosaurs that walked Earth.

The large and terrifying *Tyrannosaurus* hunted and scavenged on the large herds of plant-eating dinosaurs that roamed these wetlands. Fossils of *Triceratops* show evidence that these frilled, horned

A Tyrannosaurus (1) *is injured by a* Triceratops (2) *as it defends a juvenile. An* Ankylosaurus (3) *and a herd of* Pachycephalosauruses (4) *run from the danger.* Dracorexes (5) *hide in the undergrowth as a* Quetzalcoatlus (6) *searches for prey or **carrion**.*

dinosaurs were attacked by *Tyrannosaurus*. The armored dinosaur *Ankylosaurus* used its large tail club to protect itself from tyrannosaur attacks. Large herds of bone-headed *Pachycephalosauruses* used speed to evade predators, as did the smaller bone-headed *Dracorex*. Flying above looking for carrion was one of the largest pterosaurs to have lived, *Quetzalcoatlus*.

Quetzalcoatlus had a wingspan of 52 feet (15.8 m) and weighed around 500 pounds (227 kg).

Dinosaur Park

The warm, **temperate** coastal lowlands along the western margin of the Western Interior Seaway made ideal conditions for the formation of fossils when the animals died. Fossils of a huge variety of dinosaurs and other animals were laid down 70 million years ago in what is today known as the Dinosaur Park Formation.

Dromaeosaurus, a **theropod** the size of a wolf, hunted along the shores of the rivers and lakes. Prey included the fast-running **omnivores**

On a cliff above a lake, Struthiomimuses (1) *run from a* Dromaeosaurus (2). *Below them, a herd of* Parasaurolophuses (3) *drink from the lake as a herd of* Corythosauruses (4) *join them.* Stegocerases (5) *run along the beach in front of three* Styracosauruses (6).

Struthiomimus and *Ornithomimus* and perhaps the small bone-headed dinosaur *Stegoceras*. Frilled, horned dinosaurs such as *Styracosaurus*, *Centrosaurus*, and *Chasmosaurus* lived alongside large herds of the duck-billed dinosaurs *Corythosaurus* and *Parasaurolophus*. These dinosaurs had strange crests that may have been used to create sounds for communication.

Corythosaurus grew to 29 feet (8.8 m) long and weighed up to 4 tons (3.6 metric tons).

Two Medicines

The Two Medicine Formation was laid down in a seasonal, **semiarid** climate. This region experienced a long dry season and warm temperatures. Some of the dinosaur fossils from this time seem to show signs of **drought**-related deaths.

Two Medicine Formation is famous for its fossil eggs of *Maiasaura*, which demonstrated for the first time that at least some dinosaurs cared for their young. The eggs were arranged in dug-out earthen

At a Maiasaura (1) *nesting site, an adult cries out as a* Troodon (2) *chases a juvenile* Maiasaura. *A* Chirostenotes (3) *snatches an egg as a* Bambiraptor (4) *looks on. In the background,* Einiosauruses (5) *wander past as* Pteranodons (6) *head for feeding grounds.*

nests. Skeletons and eggs of *Troodon* were also found. Some dinosaurs like *Troodon* and *Chirostenotes* may have raided the nests, especially if they were abandoned. Fossils of a small dromaeosaurid called *Bambiraptor* were found too. It was less than 3 feet (0.9 m) long and may have been a juvenile. Also present were **ceratopsid** dinosaurs such as *Einiosaurus*, which had an unusual, downward-curving horn.

Troodon grew to 7.9 feet (2.4 m) long and weighed around 110 pounds (50 kg).

Interior Seaway

The Western Interior Seaway was a huge inland sea that split the continent of North America into two halves, Laramidia and Appalachia, during most of the Upper Cretaceous period. It was a shallow sea, filled with a huge variety of marine life.

Sea life included large predatory marine reptiles such as the plesiosaur *Elasmosaurus* and the mosasaur *Tylosaurus*. Other marine life included sharks such as *Cretoxyrhina* and advanced bony fish,

14

A Tylosaurus (1) *attacks an* Elasmosaurus (2) *feeding on ammonites (3).* Hesperornises (4) *dive after fish. Passing close by is an* Archelon (5) *and a pair of coelacanths (6). In the background, a* Cretoxyrhina (7) *lunges for a dead* Pteranodon (8).

including coelacanths. It was home to early birds also, including the flightless *Hesperornis,* which had stout legs for swimming. There were also **mollusks**, **ammonites**, squid-like **belemnites**, and **plankton**. Feeding on these as well as carrion and plants was a slow-swimming turtle the size of a car called *Archelon.*

Archelon was about 13 feet (4 m) long and weighed up to 2.2 tons (2 metric tons).

15

Giant Herds

Paleontologists in South America have dug up fossil remains of many different types of large **sauropods**. These giant dinosaurs are members of the titanosaur group, and one particular titanosaur, *Puertasaurus*, grew to a staggering 130 feet (39.6 m) long.

Living at the same time were the much smaller and more numerous titanosaurs *Saltasaurus* and *Uberabatitan*. Hundreds of fossilized *Saltasaurus* nests containing eggs have been discovered, suggesting

16

A *pair of* Austroraptors (1) *chase after* Saltasauruses (2) *with juveniles. Behind them, wandering herds of* Uberabatitans (3) *and* Puertasauruses (4) *are heading upstream for fresh water. In the foreground, a* Carnotaurus (5) *hopes to steal the* **raptors***' meal.*

that these dinosaurs lived in large herds. Fossilized skin shows that titanosaurs had bony plates providing armored protection from predators. Hunting the smaller titanosaurs were raptors such as *Austroraptor*. These large, powerful killers had long snouts containing sharp teeth. Predators such as the horned *Carnotaurus* would also have fed on titanosaurs.

Carnotaurus was about 26 feet (7.9 m) long and weighed around 2 tons (1.8 metric tons).

Smaller Giants

Running in packs, medium-sized **carnivores** like *Aucasaurus* hunted down large titanosaurs of the South American continent around 80 million years ago. Other larger predators such as *Abelisaurus* and *Aerosteon* may have hunted them alone.

The titanosaurs living at this time included *Titanosaurus*, *Pellegrinisaurus*, *Barrosasaurus*, and *Antarctosaurus*. These giant dinosaurs were not as big as *Puertasaurus* but were large enough to

A group of Aucasauruses (1) *are attempting to bring down the smaller member of a group of* Antarctosauruses (2). Uberabasuchuses (3) *flee for the safety of the river. In the distance, an* Abelisaurus (4) *chases after a* Titanosaurus (5).

put off most predators. They were plant eaters and used their long necks to reach the branches of the tallest trees. Living alongside the dinosaurs were several species of small mammals and birds such as *Patagopteryx* and *Neuquenornis*. Smaller predators such as the **crocodilian** *Uberabasuchus* inhabited the swamps and rivers, hunting smaller prey such as fish, and raiding titanosaur nests for eggs.

Antarctosaurus was about 59 feet (18 m) long and would have weighed around 37.5 tons (34 metric tons).

19

Giant Hunters

Paleontologists have discovered numerous fossils of the large predator *Mapusaurus* in one bone bed in South America. Experts suggest that these large predators probably lived and hunted together in packs to help bring down large prey such as the massively huge titanosaur *Argentinosaurus*.

Mapusaurus had a large skull with jaws filled with sharp teeth. It had very small arms and a long tail for balance. Along with *Mapusaurus*,

A group of Mapusauruses (1) are hunting down Argentinosauruses (2). A pair of Giganotosauruses (3) are following in the hope of stealing the kill. Crocodilian Araripesuchuses (4) flee from the sudden appearance of large predators.

another large carnivore, *Giganotosaurus*, hunted the large sauropods of South America. It was of similar size to *Mapusaurus* and may also have hunted in packs. Weighing in at a massive 88 tons (80 metric tons), the 120-foot (36.6 m) *Argentinosaurus* was a giant even among titanosaurs. It is more likely that the predators hunted the younger, smaller, and weaker ones instead.

Mapusaurus grew up to 41 feet (12.5 m) long and weighed 3.3 tons (3 metric tons).

African Shoreline

Along the shoreline's tidal flats, channels, and mangrove forests of Upper Cretaceous Africa lived one of the largest-ever carnivorous dinosaurs, *Spinosaurus*. Although it was a monstrous beast, it spent most of its time fishing for **aquatic** prey such as *Mawsonia*.

Spinosaurus had a crocodile-like snout with large sharp teeth ideally suited to catching its slippery prey. The spines along its back probably supported a sail-like fin that was used to regulate its temperature, much

22

An Arambourgiania (1) *launches itself from a rock as a* Stomatosuchus (2) *approaches. In the background, a* Deltadromeus (3) *follows a couple of* Aegyptosauruses (4). *In the foreground, a* Spinosaurus (5) *has just caught a* Mawsonia (6).

like a car's radiator. Alongside were the similarly large predators *Bahariasaurus* and *Carcharodontosaurus*, the titanosaur sauropods *Paralititan* and *Aegyptosaurus*, the 33-foot (10 m) crocodilian *Stomatosuchus,* and the smaller, light-footed *Dromeosaurus*. Above them, pterosaurs like *Arambourgiania*, *Alanqa*, and *Coloborhynchus* floated on the warm coastal air currents.

Spinosaurus grew up to 59 feet (18 m) long and weighed around 8 tons (7.3 metric tons).

Alioramus

Around 70 million years ago, in the flat, semiarid river plains of Upper Cretaceous Mongolia, stalked a small, primitive tyrannosaurid called *Alioramus*. Although smaller than the famous *Tyrannosaurus rex*, this lightweight predator was a ferocious hunter.

Large herds of *Saurolophuses* dominated the landscape and were likely prey to *Alioramus*. Also found on the North American continent (see pages 6–7), these large **hadrosaurid** duckbills could move on all

An Alioramus (1) *charges after three young* Deinocheiruses (2) *across a small river. A herd of* Saurolophuses (3), *startled from their feeding, get ready to run. A pair of* Therizinosauruses (4) *stop digging up termite mounds to see what's going on.*

fours or their back legs. *Alioramus* may have also hunted the large omnivorous theropod *Deinocheirus*. At 33 feet (10 m) long, it would have made a dangerous animal to take on, especially as it had long, powerful arms with sharp-clawed hands. Another dinosaur with large arms living alongside was *Therizinosaurus*. This giant omnivore had huge, **sickle**-like claws that made powerful defensive weapons.

Alioramus was around 16 feet (4.9 m) in length and weighed about 1 ton (907 kg).

Asian River Plain

On a flat plain crisscrossed with river channels, a large predator, *Tarbosaurus*, hunted the many plant-eating dinosaurs that inhabited Upper Cretaceous China.

Tarbosaurus is closely related to its North American cousin, *Tyrannosaurus*. In the humid river plain environment, it was the top predator, probably preying on other large dinosaurs like the hadrosaur *Saurolophus* (see pages 6–7 and 24–25) or *Barsboldia*. *Barsboldia* may be related to the crested duckbill *Hypacrosaurus* of North

Shantungosauruses (1) *flee from a charging* Tarbosaurus (2). *Running alongside are a couple of* Prenocephales (3) *and* Gallimimuses (4). *In the distance, a couple of* Barsboldias (5) *turn tail, while flightless* Judinornises (6) *prepare to head for deeper water.*

America. Unless injured, smaller, fleet-footed dinosaurs such as the ornithomimid *Gallimimus* and the bone-headed *Prenocephale* would have been too speedy to fall victim to large predators like *Tarbosaurus*. One of the largest of hadrosaurid dinosaurs, *Shantungosaurus*, may well have been a favorite prey to this most ferocious of Asian predators.

Shantungosaurus was only 48 feet (14.6 m) long and weighed around 18 tons (16.3 metric tons).

Asian Water Hole

One of the most amazing fossils to be discovered was found in Mongolia. It captured a *Velociraptor* and a *Protoceratops* that died together, while fighting, when they were buried as a sand dune collapsed on them.

Protoceratops were early, sheep-sized, frilled dinosaurs that lacked horns. Although they were plant eaters, the fossil shows that they could defend themselves against attack. Predators such as the dromaeosaurid *Velociraptor* were small but made up for their size by hunting in packs.

A family of Protoceratops (1) *come under attack from a pack of* Velociraptors (2). *Unseen, two* Gigantoraptors (3) *approach the fighting dinosaurs. In the foreground, a group of* Mononykus (4) *climb a log behind a lone* Citipati (5). *Overhead fly* Zhejiangopteruses (6).

A very large raptor has also been discovered in Mongolia. Called *Gigantoraptor,* this 26-foot (8 m) predator had a beaked mouth and was probably one of the fastest dinosaurs. Omnivores such as the oviraptors *Citipati* and *Mononykus* were small bipedal dinosaurs. *Mononykus* had a single claw on each arm that it used to dig out insects from rotten wood and termite nests.

Mononykus grew up to 3.3 feet (1 m) long and weighed around 10 pounds (4.5 kg).

Animal Listing

Other dinosaurs and animals that appear in the scenes.

Abelisaurus
(pp. 18–19)
Theropod dinosaur
30 feet (9.1 m)
long

Aegyptosaurus
(pp. 22–23)
Sauropod dinosaur
49.2 feet (15 m) long

Albertosaurus
(pp. 6–7)
Theropod dinosaur
29 feet (9 m) long

Ankylosaurus
(pp. 8–9)
Ankylosaurid
dinosaur
23 feet (7 m) long

Arambourgiania
(pp. 22–23)
Pterosaur
41 feet (12.5 m) ws

Araripesuchus
(pp. 20–21)
Crocodilian
6 feet (1.8 m) long

Argentinosaurus
(pp. 20–21)
Titanosaurid dinosaur
120 feet (36.6 m)
long

Aucasaurus
(pp. 18–19)
Theropod dinosaur
14 feet (4.3 m) long

Austroraptor
(pp. 16–17)

Dromaeosaurid
dinosaur
16 feet (4.9 m) long

Bambiraptor
(pp. 12–13)
Dromaeosaurid
dinosaur
3 feet (0.9 m) long

Barsboldia
(pp. 26–27)
Hadrosaurid dinosaur
35 feet (10.7 m)
long

Chirostenotes
(pp. 12–13)
Oviraptorid dinosaur
6.6 feet (2 m) long

Citipati
(pp. 28–29)
Oviraptorid dinosaur
8.9 feet (2.7 m) long

Cretoxyrhina
(pp. 14–15)
Shark
20 feet (6 m) long

Deinocheirus
(pp. 24–25)
Theropod dinosaur
33 feet (10 m) long

Deltadromeus
(pp. 22–23)
Theropod dinosaur
27 feet (8.2 m)
long

Dracorex
(pp. 8–9)
Pachycephalosaurid

dinosaur
7.9 feet (2.4 m)
long

Dromaeosaurus
(pp. 10–11)
Dromaeosaurid
dinosaur
6 feet (1.8 m) long

Einiosaurus
(pp. 12–13)
Ceratopsid dinosaur
25 feet (7.6 m)
long

Elasmosaurus
(pp. 14–15)
Plesiosaur
46 feet (14 m) long

Euoplocephalus
(pp. 6–7)
Ankylosaurid
dinosaur
23 feet (7 m) long

Gallimimus
(pp. 26–27)
Ornithomimid
dinosaur
19.7 feet (6 m)
long

Giganotosaurus
(pp. 20–21)
Theropod dinosaur
43 feet (13.1 m)
long

Gigantoraptor
(pp. 28–29)
Oviraptorid dinosaur
26.2 feet (8 m)
long

Hesperornis
(pp. 14–15)
Bird
5 feet (1.5 m) long

Judinornis
(pp. 26–27)
Bird
5 feet (1.5 m) long

Maiasaura
(pp. 12–13)
Hadrosaurid dinosaur
30 feet (9.1 m) long

Mawsonia
(pp. 22–23)
Fish
5 feet (1.5 m) long

Pachycephalosaurus
(pp. 8–9)
Pachycephalosaurid
dinosaur
23 feet (7 m) long

Pachyrhinosaurus
(pp. 6–7)
Ceratopsid dinosaur
20 feet (6 m) long

Parasaurolophus
(pp. 10–11)
Hadrosaurid dinosaur
31 feet (9.4 m)
long

Prenocephale
(pp. 26–27)
Pachycephalosaurid
dinosaur
8 feet (2.4 m) long

Protoceratops
(pp. 28–29)

Ceratopsid dinosaur
6 feet (1.8 m) long

Pteranodon
(pp. 12–13)
Pterosaur
20-foot (6 m) ws

Puertasaurus
(pp. 16–17)
Titanosaurid dinosaur
130 feet (39.6 m)
long

Saltasaurus
(pp. 16–17)
Titanosaurid dinosaur
39 feet (12 m) long

Stegoceras
(pp. 10–11)
Pachycephalosaurid
dinosaur
7 feet (2.1 m) long

Stomatosuchus
(pp. 22–23)
Crocodilian
36 feet (11 m) long

Struthiomimus
(pp. 10–11)
Ornithomimid
dinosaur
13 feet (4 m) long

Tarbosaurus
(pp. 26–27)
Theropod dinosaur
33 feet (10 m) long

Therizinosaurus
(pp. 24–25)
Theropod dinosaur
26 feet (8 m) long

Titanosaurus
(pp. 18–19)
Titanosaurid dinosaur
65 feet (19.8 m)
long

Triceratops
(pp. 8–9)
Ceratopsid dinosaur
30 feet (9.1 m) long

Tylosaurus
(pp. 14–15)
Mosasaur
49.2 feet (15 m) long

Tyrannosaurus
(pp. 8–9)
Theropod dinosaur
39 feet (12 m) long

Uberabasuchus
(pp. 18–19)
Crocodilian
10 feet (3 m) long

Uberabatitan
(pp. 16–17)
Titanosaurid dinosaur
55.7 feet (17 m)
long

Velociraptor
(pp. 28–29)
Dromaeosaurid
dinosaur
5.9 feet (1.8 m)
long

Zhejiangopterus
(pp. 28–29)
Pterosaur
11.4 feet (3.5 m)
ws

Glossary

abelisaurids Two-legged, carnivorous dinosaurs that lived in Gondwana.

ammonite An extinct sea animal with a shell that looks similar to today's nautilus.

ankylosaurid Member of the *Ankylosaurus* family of armored, plant-eating dinosaurs.

aquatic Living in water.

belemnite Squid-like sea creature.

carnivore Meat-eating animal.

carrion The remains of dead animals.

ceratopsid A member of a beaked dinosaur family.

crocodilian Group including crocodilians and their extinct relatives.

diversity A range of different things.

dromaeosaurid Small to medium-sized, feathered, carnivorous theropod dinosaurs.

drought When a region receives little or no rain and the land dries up.

ecosystem An area where plants, animals, landscape, and climate all interact.

elasmosaurs Air-breathing marine lizards.

fossil The remains of living things that have turned to rock.

hadrosaurid Duck-billed dinosaurs.

herbivore Plant-eating animal.

juvenile An individual that has not yet reached its adult form.

mass extinction event A large-scale disappearance of species of animals and plants in a relatively short period of time.

mollusk A member of the animal group that include snails, squid, and octopus.

mosasaurs Large marine lizards.

omnivore An animal that eats both meat and plants.

ornithomimids Theropod dinosaurs that looked like modern ostriches.

oviraptorid A group of bird-like dinosaurs with parrot-like beaks.

pachycephalosaurid Dinosaurs that had a domed, thick-boned skull.

paleontologist A scientist who studies earlier forms of life by looking at fossils.

plankton Minute organisms that live in water and act as food for dinosaurs.

predator An animal that hunts and kills animals for food.

pterosaur A flying reptile.

raptor Bird-like, carnivorous dinosaurs with large, scythe-like claws on their feet.

sauropod A member of a group of plant-eating dinosaurs that had very long necks.

semiarid An area of very little rainfall that can still support some plant life.

sickle A curve-bladed cutting tool.

temperate Region where seasonal changes are not extreme.

therizinosaurid A member of the plant-eating theropod dinosaurs with long, clawed hands.

theropod A member of a two-legged dinosaur family that included most of the giant carnivorous dinosaurs.

titanosaurid A member of a group of sauropod dinosaurs.

tyrannosaurid Member of the *Tyrannosaurus* family of carnivorous theropod dinosaurs.

Index